Visiting Days

Poems

Gretchen Primack

Willow Books
Detroit, Michigan

Visiting Days: Poems

Editor: Randall Horton

Cover design: Nancy Leonard

ISBN 978-1-7322091-4-5

LCCN 2018961863

Editor's Choice Series

Willow Books, a Division of Aquarius Press

www.WillowLit.net

Printed in the United States of America

For the caged

…siempre olvido que soy

real…

…I often forget that I am

real…

Table of Contents

Acknowledgments

Some of these poems have appeared in:

Glass: A Journal of Poetry ("Knowledge (East Wing)," ("Knight (East Wing)")

Hanging Loose ("Ben (South Hall)," "Guinness (East Wing)," "Rifle (South Hall)")

Indianola Review ("Ismail in the Laundry," "Manuel (South Hall)")

Like Light: 25 Years of Poetry & Prose, Bright Hill Press ("Hawk (North Hall)," "Hector (South Hall)")

Little Patuxent Review ("Ingrid (Visiting Room)")

Poet Lore ("Abdullah (West Wing)," "Shawn (North Hall)," "RH (North Hall)")

Project Intersect ("The Caged")

Red Wheelbarrow ("Ernest (Vocational)," "Deneice (Trailer Visit)," "David (East Wing)," "Hector (South Hall)")

Spoon River Poetry Review ("Correction," "Addiction")

Tinker Street ("Jeremy (Bullpen)," "Hakim (The Box)")

Watershed Review ("Andre Going Home," "Majestic On His Way," "Marcus (B3)," "King (The Yard)")

The voices in this book are imaginary, but I have benefitted tremendously from working with incarcerated men and women. Great thanks to those at the New York State prisons who inspired and/or contributed, especially Joe Bergamini, Arlander Brown, Gordon Davis, Josh Horein, Paul Kim, Darren Mack, Javier Miranda, Anthony Perez, Monique Robertson, Alphonso Simmons, Angel Tueros, and Tony Singh. An extra-emphatic thank you to Jule Hall and Robert Riggs.

Thanks also to the following authors whose writings were helpful: Michelle Alexander, Jimmy Santiago Baca, Reginald Dwayne Betts,

Eldridge Cleaver, Michael S. Collins, Angela Y. Davis, Curtis Dawkins, Rene Denfeld, Atul Gawande, Donna Hylton, Randall Horton, Franz Kafka, Etheridge Knight, Jarvis Jay Masters, Seth Michelson, John Mingo, William A. Noguera, Matthew Parker, Bruce Scottus Reilly, Gresham Sykes, and Judith Tannenbaum. Thanks to Noah McClain and Robert Riggs for their sociological work. The following anthologies were also helpful: *Rough Draft Vols. I and II*, edited by Bard Prison Initiative students; *No Fixed Place on Earth: An Anthology of Words + Art*, The Alabama Prison Arts + Education Project; *Women Making History: Writings from the U.S. Women's History Class*, Camp Beacon Women's Correctional Facility; and *The Untold Story of the Real Me: Young Voices from Prison*, Free Minds Book Club and Writing Workshop.

I am grateful to fellow writers whose support has meant so much: Bruce Beasley, Celia Bland, Jody Bolz, Kia Corthron, Ruth Danon, Judith Kerman, Joan Larkin, Wendy Wilder Larsen, Tom Lux (RIP), E. Ethelbert Miller, Joseph Ross, Vijay Seshadri, Tim Seibles, Truth Thomas, Jean Valentine, Dayl Wise, David Wright, and David Young.

Finally, deep gratitude to Randall Horton, for believing so strongly in this book; Heather Buchanan, who brought it into the world; and Gus Mueller, who walks with me through that world.

Introduction

I have seven felony convictions. I have been to that place you refer to as prison, a term I refuse to use anymore because society imprisoned me long before prison, but no more. Call it freedom of the no longer spellbound. I did five years on the inside. I have seen the unimaginable, over and over. I have witnessed stabbings by shank and suicide by hanging from a knotted sheet from the top tier. My former cellmate was raped and had to check into protective custody. I don't have to guess what the inside looks like, what it tastes like, what it feels like nor what it smells like because I can, and always will be able to, reproduce a cage habitat from memory. But I have also witnessed humanity, kindness, compassion—people willing and wanting to change, if given the chance. This is what I know: if you come to the inside looking for a stereotype, you will find it.

Enter Gretchen Primack, a poet, writer and advocate who dismisses the stereotype and is able to see the humanity in the people that touched her life on the inside. The conversation often arises within advocacy debate as to who has the license to contribute to this conversation, especially through art and creative expression. *Visiting Days* by Gretchen Primack is a prime example of how to get it right. This is a brave and necessary collection of poems that contribute to the overall debate around the criminal justice system, and more specifically the prison industrial complex, with all its complexities.

In the age of cultural correctness, sometimes to a fault (a box will always be a box no matter how it is reshaped for the sake of a feelgood), we want to challenge those who step outside of their comfort zone to totally immerse themselves in that which they write about. Gretchen has done this with great care and detail. She is a poet who takes the task of poeting seriously: art for the sake of art. Even before you read the following pages, know that people from the inside have laid eyes on this manuscript, and each one was awed that someone not of their world took the time to understand their plight in a way that rendered them human. A person I know who spent considerable time on the inside put it like this: "When you go to court, you don't mind a lawyer representing you, even though the lawyer does not share your experience." Primack is here to help, has put in over twenty years of unselfish work to get to this point, to tell these invisible stories through other people's voices.

Make no mistake, I will always fight for those living at ground zero to have a voice, and at Willow Books, that is what we are doing: being proactive. *Visiting Days* sets the stage for a series of poetry chapbooks and collections authored by women on the inside. As editors, Heather Buchanan and myself are committed to and believe art can be transformational, that it must, at times, deal with the difficult, that it must make you uncomfortable in ways you could have never imagined. If you feel a little uncomfortable about this book, then we (Willow Books and Gretchen Primack) have done our job as both publisher and poet.

Randall Horton

Senior Editor

Ismail (Laundry)

There is a musk that won't boil off
in bleach. A white

yellow as an old eye.
There is a sound like a train

juddering under the river,
pushing through with its forehead,

pushing through my forehead.
And I fold.

Sisyphus knows this room
and the mess line down

the hall and the line behind
the swinging kitchen door.

He knows these net bags
full of green. The skin of us,

a green not found in nature,
our DINs above the pocket:

the number on our green skins
sealed in cinderblock.

No one wants what is
state issue. Most is state issue.

And I fold. And push the canvas
on its tired black wheels.

What you can wear non-state:
Solid red. Solid yellow. Purple. No

blue, no orange. No patterns.
No black.

Damon (B3)

It was a smaller sun than usual
so we stayed in bed tangled
with skinny cats and demons.
I was low. You were high as a small
moon, so I went high as a harsh sun,
full of foul anthems unleashed
on the world. *What a waste,*
I kept thinking, *all this talk*
of God. I burned high and red until
bracelets circled my wrists like small
moonlights, behind my back
where I can't see them.

Jeremy (Bullpen)

And in the towers of Attica—no—
in the bowels of Attica, my
mask came down, the acetylene fired,
and the joint that set leg to brace
welded just so, and I fit the drawers
just so, and took my perk showers.
Somewhere, a contract flurried here

to there, and the desk I made was packed
by men on my company, and shipped
south, set by a wall of windows
in the Freedom Tower.

Correction

I

"No, not *live*," she says. "They *lock*."
She wears blue and they wear green:
Blue is I live in town, green
is I lock at the prison, I have done wrong, I am probably
brown, probably black, you are blue and white,
you have done good.

Ben wears green, he locks, he is white.
He paints ripe fantasies, realism that needs
a kick from a drunk post-impressionist.
Ben locks, he aced Numbers Theory,
wears green, likes Kant. Karim loves
Hegel, he locks, he is black, his German
is fluent, born of Hegel, he wears green.

Manuel loves Cuba in all its Raul, he is brown
wearing green, he reads all night where he locks.
He writes poems, he plays guitar
where he locks. He orates in Spanish,
in English, either and both like his poemas.

Egan wears blue, he is white, he lives
because he is good. He likes guns and Trumps,
likes writing up people in green,
people who lock, writing tickets on them,
likes hands wide on the wall
and green legs apart. There are Karim's legs
and hands apart.

II

You are a junkie murderer, a murdering pimp,
a pimp junkie. A dealer, assailant,
extortionist, persistent felon, who knows what.
This place is ugly because you are
ugly. You need an ugly place to host your
ugliness, Manuel of the wide broken smile, small
terror.

It went down when he was sixteen.
Something terrible. His brain's rills weren't done.
What lives did he spoil while they took
shape?

Now he is thirty-six.

III

How many times have I looked
up at that in all its phases,
the dim and less dim, slivers and coins,
smooth expanses, pocks,
and never once through bars.

How many times have I held my breath
at the mercy of muses and given myself
quiet to help them come,
and there you are, Manuel, with the yard
shrieking up to the wind by your window,
and next cell's static, other side's howl,
and the booming cops, and now lights
or chow or no lights and a cell toss
and ticket while the yard spills
through the wind in the window grate.

IV

Manuel sits on a hard bed,
commissary notebook open.
A beam of lamp not bought
but issued. Sounds that limestone
and sand make. The commissary pen
uncaps, and the words muscle in,
all elbows. Some are bread nuts
half cracked. Some are waste solder
still warm from the iron. Some
are bitter fishes.

A whole government of fog passes
his window grate. The fog, the pen,
the notebook put wedding rings
on all his fingers. Inside his head,
fists open into flat hands, somebody's.
They smell of blue burning. Of her
quinceañera. Of bitter copper and
browned bread nuts lying
on their sides.

V

Jacob is black and wears green,
and from his yard bench he looks
at a fence and thinks, If I were ten,
that would be something to climb.
To climb over and then forget.

Now it doesn't matter what there is
to learn, he yearns to learn it,
to eat its paper. Thinking
is something to climb
and love the climbing of. Dylan
Thomas, Thomas Eliot,
George Eliot, Thompson's *George II*,
the Second Law of Thermodynamics:
Entropy. The Second Law of Motion:
Force, Mass, Movement.

He was twenty when it went down.
Now he is forty. What he has not done
since twenty: Sat in an armchair.
Submerged in water.
Ordered lunch.
Looked at a moon
in quiet.

Jacob bends his head over Emerson.
Jacob of the rare smile.
He points, another bad man bends over,
a black man in green.
A chief event of life is the day in which
we have encountered a mind that startled us
by its large scope.

Jacob points at Manuel's tattered
Amichai. The words are bridge
and fire at once.
The words climb up and over
and rattle on the road. *Here
is the road and the going on it,
what does it mean?*

David (East Wing)

Nothing was normal about it, the cars we slept in, the crack
they smoked that smoked them.

Then I met him, and he fed me for the first time: a mother.
He took me out safely: A father.

Dragged his hand along my cheek
without even touching me: a mother.

He saw the violence in my bed
and moved me to the foot of his: A savior.

I owed him my life, which those who value a bed,
a cupboard, a ceiling understand.

He became my father mother savior brother, which those
who value their own bodies understand. And I gave him

the violence he asked of me, an almost-man who needed
a father to save him from his father, a brother to save him

from that father's brother, a savior who saw what happened
at night. Of course I did what he wanted, trembling like a bastard.

The storm of materials of me safeguarding him in violence.
What he asked for through his lens, what I did through mine.

William (Phones)

A brown moth is on its way from my block
to her dirty snow. Takes its time
sometimes. The butcher calling
his house above the butcher shop.
And here comes back a tough old butterfly,
nicked wing, orange almost burnt.
Her salt breath calls to me, calls out
what she calls me: son, *my son.*

Clinic

One morning you notice your stool
is marbled with mucous and blood.
The doctor says he'll get to you and
sends you off. But every day, runny,
viscous, bloody stool, so after three
weeks, you return to the clinic and
are chastised for your impatience:
there are patients with real problems.

Five more weeks pass before a
popsicle stick test reveals your
acute and contagious infection.
Clostridium difficile does not play.
You're sent to isolation for ten days
with the clothes you have on. The
contents of your cell are disposed
of or sent away. Two months after
treatment, you're still hoping for
a second pair of pants.

Knowledge (East Wing)

I honor life by not taking it anymore. Not a fish's life.
Not a calf's. No one's brother or child.

I did violence. I put it between my teeth
and it formed my blood, and I took blood.

Now I eat what they ate in Eden before violence.
Now I ask forgiveness for the life I've taken

that wasn't mine to take—the man, and the calves
and fishes, the chicks and their mothers.

The cops laugh. Their work is domination.
They lord over, and some men on the block

call themselves kings. But I am done with that
in every soul of me, every body.

Ingrid (Visiting Room)

The woman who won't shut up, the kid whose eyes cross,
the couple old as Moses with their slip-on shoes and clear bag
of dollars. We all go straight for the vending machines, Swiss
steaks enrobed in plastic for her, Swiss & turkey sub for him,
must be something about the Alps.

What if the guard told a joke that was funny? There was a jumble
of high chairs in that corner when I got here, now just one
facing the wall, the wall an under-the-sea mural, all of us fish
in air. The choking poster rolls its eyes above the Bible table.

Now the men come through, one of them you, and check in
at the guard's double chin, like everyone, like always,
and like always for a moment I can't look up.

Knight (East Wing)

Poisoned water, poisoned sleep
ground under the heel of my pillow.
If I didn't know your cell song,
I would think I tread the red
circle alone.

But Etheridge, I found you
here, and I have rolled
myself up in your night speech,
so I know something good
come out of prison.

And I have pressed against
the western wall, so I know
you saw through stone.

It's not visions in my cell,
never those. Tony hung
from his sheet and I see him.
I see the bars cut the tensed cloth
into pieces across from me.
But not as visions.

And I'd like to report to you,
Sir Knight who gifted me
a name:
            Sometimes the wind rings
in this ear and then the other,
but this poetman will die
as trumpets.

Something good come out
of prison.

Samuel (North Hall)

In the fall, dead leaves shape into a rug and I can breathe,
seeing a cover. In winter the snow.

There are no rugs here. No cloths.
Nothing soft. Chilled surfaces.

But in the fall the leaves
toss down a rug and I can breathe, seeing

a cover. In winter the snow.

Ernest (Vocational)

"The materials produced by the Mattress Shop are standard items
used in state and local facilities and universities throughout
the state."
—NYS Department of Corrections

Education is part of this. For instance: I had to get my GED.
And for instance: my work will lie under a student
at Buffalo State. On my clothed buttons lie students
about to get laid, students dreaming of books
and getting laid. Dreaming of stories and science. Never
of their mattress. Never of its tufting machine operator,
or tape edge operator, never of its felon. Its spring mattress
assembler. Its twenty-to-life adhesive operator, cutting
machine operator, conditional-release-2023 mattress
sewing machine operator, its GED-2012 stuffing machine
operator, its man.

Jacob (School Building)

A healthy soul stands…to all beholders like a transparent object betwixt them and the sun, and whoso journeys toward the sun, journeys toward that person.
—R. W. Emerson

I pack my mind with more
and more and then it will be laid
in the ground with the rest of me.

I see that fence out the meshed
window and think, once upon a time,
that was something to climb.

I didn't mind the ones the army
set up for me. They kept me honorable
until discharge.

This one can't do that, not when
I could hustle here
hard as the street.

But I'm not young.
I want to breathe pages and chapters
and afterwords.

I didn't want the army like that.
I didn't want my children like that.

I didn't feel my healthy soul
until these pages, and now

my soul hums, brims
over, in its journey.

Petey (The Box)

As if colors.

As if brutal.

Sometimes the rolling.
Basket of it. Sometimes
the shrink if it.

Tell it to always. Try to all the time.
And whether.

It smells tired.

Something threaded
and buried.

M, m, m, mine
my may me.

Telling the wall
what to say back.

As if tired out
and nothing touching.

Under lights
nothing not lights

and nothing touching.

Justice (East Wing)

I started at Downstate, like everybody, in '84. Then I was packed up for Coxsackie for four years. Then Shawangunk for two, then Clinton for one, Greenhaven for three. Clinton again for one, and then Elmira for one. No, Elmira then Clinton. Then back to Greenhaven for two, then Upstate SHU, then Hudson SHU, back to Coxsackie for one. Then Eastern for five, and now I'm on the draft for Woodbourne.

Capp (B3)

All body
on the
court and
the hoop is
a free thing
above every
thing, a tall
and iron reiner-
in. My body
makes it shiver
when I clutch it.
The ball is a free
thing that can
take in ground,
take in air, clear
fences, be lost
to me and
everyone. My
body makes
the ball tremble
when I palm it,
is a balm
when I stuff it.
All body in
the flaking light,
a body bluing
its veins, bluing
its lungs, a hoop
and free air,
sweat turning
to powder when
the body turns
joints joined

in grace, moving
blood that
moves
like grace.

Papa G (B3)

Fathers are allowed to not love.
I loved anyway.

He was a moment that made my heart
announce itself.

But he slipped under the black rock
as if I'd never loved at all.

Took time but I found that devil
who pushed him under.

Found him and I pushed him
under, his mouth round as zero,

I pushed him so far under the world
his body was hardly found.

They found me
guilty. I found me.

Addiction

lies tangled in your gut
like undone knitting,

smells strong as
an undressed orange.

Walks over the
undug pit of you.

It sweats under synthetics,
under your inked-up rind,

a hearty germ,
the stink of bones.

You were young and there
was first after first.

Sometimes you were
walking on the ground,

sometimes the Earth,
everything running

around you: marching bands,
town halls, rocket ships.

Then there was rage,
a sudden fang thrill.

Then the afterward, duller
than rage. Torqueless, no

drama, no deathbed wisdom.
And all these chances we have,

minute after minute,
to kill ourselves.

And all this language
more dead than alive,

drained of power, weak keys
fitting weak locks all

over town. News weak,
sex, even death with

its endless tubes,
its metal hearts ticking

straight through
to underground.

So you took poison
into the small house

of you, lay it tangled
in your gut like undone

knitting, packed it into
your bitter chest.
.

Senate (South Hall)

I don't feel like it tonight,
what it takes, the dim twist
of this non-life of Life.

And on every wall the broken and
broken down muscle of his chest,
how I made his end.

And the pride and gorge in my throat.
The gall and pride in my throat,
its syrup and acid on every wall.

In the steel pane where my face lives
lives his face. He was a child
too. The beef meant everything.
What does it mean now
in this polished steel.

Hear me, paper.
Feel me, pen.
If I'm not asleep,
I hurt.

In the steel pane where my face lives
lives his face.

We were children.
What does the beef mean
now, in this polished steel.

Someone's end and a tired
face locked down and up.
Broken.

Jolon (Night Rec)

The games, tricks, catchin rec,
word play make me laugh half
the time. Make me whole
sometimes. Could kill me with
their serious, their hurt, words
rolling off the spool from his mouth
to my expense.

These are the ways stories keep me alive
in their textures
or char my skin in them.

One sly tale taller
than another—how we like it.
Things that can't be tamped:
the fluttering card shuffle
and language that could get
me murdered, could get me
crippled for days. Could save
my life and my manhood.

Brother, don't try this
where it wouldn't save your life.

Deneice (Trailer Visit)

Honeymoon with the smallest moon
shape and no honey, and still this room
is full of beams and honey. We are
a couple coupling, and I am a wife
lying down with you for the first time.
And staring. How that lash corner brushes
the thin pillow, how your cheek darkens
against the white case. The pots
are battered but hold a love's worth
of noodles, and this bed is big enough
for two: A change for you. In it I get
to touch you alone for the first time
and tell you about all the parts inside
of me, the ones you can feel and
the ones you can't. In nine years
eight months ten days we will do this
with no clocks.

KT (The Box)

I have a sign because I was born
under one, but no omens.
Just because you think in here,
doesn't mean it matters, no matter
who you are. And me: No Malcolm,
no Mandela, no Susan B.

Time passes with no effort
from me or anyone else, whether
we mark it, tear it out of the tile,
press its hand. The earth
makes men out of bones
and cells every day.
The earth makes bones
out of men every day.

And water.
The waters of my heart are brackish
today, the swamp of my little years
far from here and behind me.
I wanted saving but the water
wasn't sweet enough,
the air was too thick, I would
have needed more wind,
a different skin
to be stuffed into.

Now, as then, I am unaccounted for
in the world, have no numbers
attached. In 1815, 1915, 2015,
flour and grease have done
the same work, the moon smells
the same, the Law is the same
murk.

The air is thin in this north.
The waters dry quick. I've been salted
and cured. I've been wrapped tight,
and the door is tight on its hinge.
I may never see my swamp, never
again spend my time weaving
among citizens and their time.
Do they want saving?
Are they saved?

Hakeem (The Box)

Cell of dead cells my cells crawl cells sleep cells knife
cells blood cells nerve cells froze blood cells soup cells
most ghost cells god cells air cells her cells hell cells
sting cells stone cells throb cells sky cells
    red cells sick
cells blood cells red blood cells black cells hole cells
cell cells ma cells lost cells brown cells lost green
cells sad cells hell cells cell hell

The Caged

The chickens, stuffed
ten to one. The felons.
The beagles stuffed with
drain clearer, the pot dealers,
the pot smokers. The calves
chained neck to door,
the transports chained
wrist to ankle, the rapists,
the turkeys in fall. The *No*
*I Didn't*s, the bait dogs,
the dog fighters, the breeding
sows, the egg layers. The
murderers, the convicted
innocents, the convicted,
the innocents.

Guinness (East Wing)

Rage could wrap around the earth's middle and squeeze
until the poles pop
    and where should I feel it
it could stand on a hammer's head on the nail in the
Savior's hand
    and where should I let it out
it could melt the tongue out of the sun's mouth
and where should I slough it—
this cinderblock corner maybe
industry maybe chow
the hall to medical or medical maybe
but no of course
nowhere—not here in feral close smells and the same
and same and the hollow
close sounds
 a city of rage and its chemicals
 in me   a country of it
poison on both sides of my skin and nowhere to

Majestic on His Way

Every tenth body in green walks by
in white skin.
Every tenth body in blue
walks by in brown skin.

On our way to mess, seas split
around civilians: the named
among the numbered,
pastors and teachers and workmen

parting the brown sea.
There they go, into the pastor's
promised land, the teacher's
hallowed halls, the workman's

deep toolbox. The brown sea seals
behind them and their white
escorts. Our tributary twists to mess,
its line of forks and cups, the line
in all its colors.

Hector (South Hall)

Between your sleeping teeth,
Mama, the ghost
of a sentence,
a life one,
mine.

All the stories in the world
and this one is yours.
You speak in tongues
but I have only this to tell.
You were always freer than me.

I think you're in bed
with your bones and tongue
asleep. I think the radio
is on, sticky with waffle syrup.
I think the coffee maker once
again nests roaches as free
as you are.

Out your window is the boardwalk
on a sea full of bitter fishes,
a shore of killed birds. How many
times did I drink with them
while you slept free.
How many fogs away are you.

Ten fogs away, your tongue
sleeps in its crook while the lonely
light of lightning spends itself
as hard as it can.

Honey (North Hall)

They need to move me to Bedford because what is a man? How long
am I me before I am seen?
I was a little woman as a little man, let my little woman be known
a little here a little there, mama saying *be gay but don't be girl.*

I came north, the sag of Jacksonville pulled up with my hair.
I pinned my hair up in a sweep of Queens and tangled in my tricks.
I was no man to them or me.
I tangled in smack, went helpless in its damp.

Now the church turns its cinderblock back. Now the ballers
and card players stand when I sit. Now the guards call me *it*,
call me *thing*, shove me to the wall and the bed with lust and disgust.

When I am free, I will go under the knife. And all of these cut pages,
smile after shine on my walls, will show who I am. And lasers til I'm
smooth as my womanhood, every follicle clear and buried.

And no habit. Now I'm afraid to think but sometimes feel anyway.
But when I am free,
no habit, because who needs a habit when she is free?

JR (Chapel)

I can't

say

I know

You,

but

I know

what You

have done:

made me

a seen

man.

Made me

a

harmony line.

Seen me

and

sung

me: A candle

drying

in its own

heat.

A sorry

black wick.

I know

your

smell—

clean

burning

and light

on skin

for

the first

time.

Hawk (North Hall)

You cannot promote free will…by extinguishing it.
—Bruce Western

A whistling hollow passes
as you pass another citizen
in the street. The whistling
hollow a dead soul makes, or
a me-shaped hole not
on its way to create
in the world. Not allowed
to create in the world.
And what will rush
into that vacuum?

What if I am
worthy, not danger.
I am denied you. And
you don't know
who you are
without me.

What if my will
would bend
toward citizen.
What if I would do
out there like you do.
Better.

Ben (South Hall)

I had enough taken from me but I have this charcoal
and these pencils, now contraband but for me
grandfathered. Heirlooms.

My delight on paper. My arm is State green
but at the end of it is a moving hand and
it colors, making a hand

the color of my hand. Escher loved ordering,
non-Euclidian geometries, regular and irregular
divisions of the plane,

the nature of space. I love ordering, non-Euclidian
geometries, tessellations, the nature of space.
My arm is dressed

in State greens, but my hand is dressed in charcoal
and pencil, and I can move my wrist and pencil
any ways I please and make

my order. Even the cop at his desk is mine
to order, a shape on a sketchpad, three lines,
a flick, shading.

This morning he fastened a blue shirt
over his hollow chest, he buttoned his white
buttons one by one.

Now on my pad, he is a man whose hollow
chest is cut open for all to see.

Abdullah (The Box)

Someone chewed up moons and spit them out
up there. The wind, the leaves, two machines
in two places down there, the wind, dry sticks. The clouds alive
for a change. I can put my skull on this pillow
all night and they will be out there,
quiet-alive. The gold machines will shift places
by noon, chewing earth up and spitting it out.

West Wing Inmate

I surrender matches hidden shallow
so I can keep the lighter hidden deep

West Wing Guard

I let the matches go
so I can take the lighter

Shawn (North Hall)

I believe that the number of trees I see out there together
means *forest.* I believe forests have paths and small
moss under the trees. I believe leaves grind
into thick powder on the paths. I believe spiders live there,
that they string their lines between trees.
That if I were there walking the powder would feel
hollow, that a spider string would break across my chest
like a finish-line ribbon, bad for the spider and for me,
the gluey catch on my chest.

Edgar (West Wing)

Smack. It's why I lock in, it's why
the street dreams. But who wouldn't want to feel
his eyes snug into bones, skin snug itself
into a soft jacket, hearing fitting snug;
who wouldn't want to watch it solve the world,
and make hair feel functional, dull feel matte,
make the cat puzzle-piece your lap
joints, waste nothing, fit into a nest,
make breath ink, make breath fill time,
breath coating clean inside the lungs,
almost a caress, almost a death,
the kind that makes relief a killing rain;
the spoon and me run such a simple meld…
positions can be held and held and held….

Frank (B3)

I can tell from the letters you are a good fuck   a tight one
and how I would fuck you   start with your mouth   a yellow bite
on your neck   red bites on your breast   red bites
on your hip and cunt   and I would drag you tight   drive your
thighs apart   far as they go   harpoon you   drag you even clos-
er
skid you clear across the room   stutter the bed   gouge
the floor   gouge you   and I would come like a fire   like
a storming   I would come all orange   all salt oceans
bigger than religions   every one

Marcus (B3)

Dust the rain kicks up from
cement looks like your angel
breath and smells like smoke
over a construction site,
its ordered mayhem,
the smoke falling through
my ribs, the ordered mayhem
you have made of me.

Keeplocked, windows
are everything.
A kid, I ate in the dark.
A teen, I drank outside.
A teen, I came here and here
I am, a man.

But where would we have met
but here? You help me be here
because you are precious
and you are here.

War of the heart.
They want to deny me
just what saves me here.
Here, where I am to be saved.
We are not allowed, love.
And so: Resistance.
Just what these wall spur
in me is what they want
to crush.

But this is where you
gathered me in

and all the chambers
of you called out warm,
"You are, we are."

Rifle (South Hall)

Time moves here,
too. The first sunburn
at my new hairline.
An inch of crow's feet.
Everyone around me
the same and joking
through with me.
The yard is littered
with tobacco we clear
from cigar shells
for blunts while our jaws
slack and stretch the slack
with laughing and hollers.
The yard is littered with blunt
ash and my sister marries.
All of us heal somewhere
on the body while
the crow's feet creep
and my father goes under
the knife. My cells slow
and I play through,
how we do,
our war stories
and cards.

Gilbert (B3)

For Emily

I wish I'd met you—in your room—
as quiet as a bee
whose days were almost over—
no pollen left to say—

I'm in my room and told—like you—
my meanings aren't real
though maybe in a hundred years
they'll gather I could feel—

and come to find a hundred bids
from hundreds in like me—
a cast of castaways in bed
with acid history.

I want your music—quiet one.
Unwarm my fever-skin!
So odd—remarkable—delicate
the case your mind was in—

Lyon (B3)

what I've learned is
how forgiving my skin is

what others have done

what I have done

and still it stretches back over
the drum of me

the beating
beaten drum.

Roman (North Hall)

All I ask is a way to create something from nothing
here. A field and hoe so I can bring forth cabbage,
a sketch, a tune or a love note.
Which I do. This ground is shot through
with mines and shrapnel, but some of us work it
anyway, and sometimes this mantling and dismantling,
earthing and unearthing unearths the runnels
of life, its cold and warm fruits. Cabbage
and tall peas. The grounding notes
of a guitarrón. Swapping portraits
for commissary, every sketch a green vine
snaking the minefield and living. Every measure
a lead shard buried deeper where it can't hurt.

.

.

Karim (School Building)

The pursuit of knowing was freedom to me.
—Ta-Nahisi Coates

That man at the whiteboard,
Columbia, children,
sidewalks: He is why my German
ist recht gut. His Nietzsche, the way
he sat Hegel down with me.

Some ideas prevail. You don't
have to agree with them
to love them. You only have
to love their transmission:
That they did in the world.
That they did to the world.
You only have to love
what it means to prevail.

Hegel: *The learner always begins*
by finding fault, but the scholar
sees the positive merit in everything.

You only have to love their searches.
I have loved searching those.
I have loved that like food.
I have loved those like the absence
of doors.

Jero (Visiting Room)

My daddy say Allah know everything.
Daddy here every time I come. He
tell me You my little boy and he call me
Little Man. Sometime I call him Big
Man back. He like that. He used to
say Jesus die for me. Mama cry
when we come but I don't.
Daddy know everything.

RH (Visiting Room)

What kind of father wants his son to run?
Run. Tear the page in half. I'm in your jaw,
the way you move your small elbows
across from me. You are in all of me. Find
what's clean. Your mother's house,
her love in your throat each night,
my love in the flickering bulb on the landing.
My air could choke you like blue dirt
packed. Don't come back.

My cogs are jammed with grease,
limned with rust rime you'd sand
your hands on. That is how ugly
I am inside. Find what's clean.
Your mother's hands.

A train car is neutral until the locomotive
hooks on and drags it to its will,
stinking of grease and bones.
This is not your track, child.

King (The Yard)

On the outside, sun and reality shrink people back to their actual size. In here, people grow into their shadows.
—Rene Denfeld

When the cloud bottoms turn to fish bellies
I leave the yard.

A yard is where our plastic pool sat
in Far Rockaway. That can't

have happened.
That it happened

saves me every night.
There are always shadows

in this yard, on the courts
and benches, cement pockets,

the armory wall. Shadows of
every shade, wherever

the sun is, the dark. Darker.
Darkest. The filmed-over.

Trees cracking their knuckles
in wind.

Black air rushing in
where the sun's air

doesn't want to be.
Every shade. Men

and their shadows,
whatever the clouds do,

whatever I've done,
the shadows rush into

any space,
spaces are stuffed

with them, so that
I must make

as little space
as I can.

7-Up (East Wing)

Last night, a dream: Dialysis for every organ.
Instead of three times a week in the clinic,
I'm there on the hour. Bile filters mechanically
through my liver, gall through my gall bladder.
Mechanical air pumps my lungs open and shut.
Saline cranks across my lenses.

Now it is time for the clinic.
One day, I will gather the tubes
and filters and climb into a coffin,
settle them in beside me on the way
to the potter's field.

Kao Dreams of an Ocean (West Wing)

A wooden ship, a grace
of salt from aft.

Stars shoving themselves
through the paint.

This is a black pan gliding.
A black cup cupping water.

Dimpled salted water,
troubled with fishes.

And here is
Captain Me.
Ocean, captain me.

Such a different blue.
Not a captor
but a captivator.

The earth's skin.
My chest humming
like a treasure chest.

My chest upended
with its slumped heart,

its shakes like a bay
in ripple.

Fathoms coated by a coat
thrown by a moon soaked

then dry. Fathoms I can fathom,
knots I've unknotted
atom by atom

where the water
furls and I am tested
and meet it,

as unlandlocked
as there is,
as untethered.

Andre Going Home

Knowing me as I do:
the German spirit in the black faces
of me: The black spirit in my German
bearings: I know what I will come to know
of Whitehead's *manifold frustrations*
of liberty. I know some nights
I'll want to lock in.

Some days my shoes will fill
with dread and keep me boxed.
Some nights my chest will press
against me, keep me cornered.

Some days the free will reach
out with all the mad fingers
of its body and keep me locked.

There are whole swaths of me
I haven't seen in years.
Doors, let me open you
with my exhales. Gates,
let me close you behind me
with my inhales. Street,
let me be too unimportant
to ruin again.

Manuel (South Hall)

What mis palabras do
is give me back fruit

*

What image does is keep
me a father

*

What assonance is:
consonance
*

Words jewel me
on all my fingers

*

The sound of words
their apariencia
how they mean in my tongue
is how I taste fruit

*

Words pull the sorrow
from every tooth.

*

What happens
is what doesn't

ankles forget to sprain
radios sound like a moth

leaves and puddles stay put

leaders sleep

*

the notebook opens
and breath is not a block
bound to my chest

it is a cloud broken open
rain broken out

Notes

The book's epigraph is from the poem "Olvido" from *Dreaming America: Voices of Undocumented Youth in Maximum-Security Detention,* edited by the poetry workshop leader, Seth Michelson (Settlement House 2017). The poets were not permitted to be named in the collection, thus the lack of attribution here.

Section III of "Correction" nods to Randall Horton's "A Reoccurring Nightmare in Maximum Security," *Of Note Magazine*, http://www.ofnotemagazine.org/2015/01/21/randall-horton.

"Knight (East Wing)" includes several phrases from *The Essential Etheridge Knight*, University of Pittsburgh Press, 1986.

The epigraph of "Hawk (North Hall)" is from Bruce Western's introduction to Gresham Sykes' *The Society of Captives: A Study of a Maximum Security Prison*, Princeton University Press, 2007. In the quoted passage, Western is paraphrasing Sykes.

The epigraph of "Jacob (School Building)" is from Emerson's essay "Character."

The epigraph of "Karim (School Building") is from Coates' *Between the World and Me*, Spiegel & Grau, 2015.

The epigraph of "Ernest (Vocational)" is from the NYS Department of Corrections website, on which they list programs available to inmates in various prisons. http://www.doccs.ny.gov/ProgramServices/vocational.html

The ending terms of "Gilbert (B3)" echo one of Thomas Wentworth Higginson's letters, in which he says Emily Dickinson's work is "remarkable, though odd . . . *too delicate*—not strong enough to publish" (Thomas H. Johnson's introduction to *The Complete Poems of Emily Dickinson*, Faber & Faber, 1975).

The epigraph of "King (The Yard)" is from Denfeld's novel *The Enchanted*, Harper, 2014.

The italics in "Andre Going Home" are a concept in Colson Whitehead's *The Underground Railroad*, Doubleday, 2016.

About the Author

Gretchen Primack is the author of two other poetry collections, *Kind* (Post-Traumatic Press) and *Doris's Red Spaces* (Mayapple Press). Her poems have appeared in *The Paris Review*, *Prairie Schooner*, *The Massachusetts Review*, *Field*, *Poet Lore*, *Antioch Review*, *Ploughshares*, and other journals. She has administrated and taught with education programs in prison and jail for many years, and moonlights at an indie bookstore in Woodstock, NY. Also an advocate for non-human animals, she co-wrote the memoir *The Lucky Ones: My Passionate Fight for Farm Animals* (Penguin Avery).

CPSIA information can be obtained
at www.ICGtesting.com
Printed in the USA
FFHW021852050319
50887592-56292FF